Language: English

These materials are designed to assist you in learning about hope. They should not be used for medical advice, counseling, or other health-related services. iFred, The Shine Hope Company and Kathryn Goetzke do not endorse or provide any medical advice, diagnosis, or treatment. The information provided herein should not be used for the diagnosis or treatment of any medical condition and cannot be substituted for the advice of physicians, licensed professionals, or therapists who are familiar with your specific situation. Consult a licensed medical professional, or call 911, if you are in need of immediate assistance.

ISBN: 978-1-7359395-6-8

© 2020, Kathryn Goetzke.

All rights reserved. No part of this book may be reproduced, shared or distributed without the written permission of the publisher. For more information, please contact kathryngoetzke@theshinehopecompany.com.

We designed The Hopework book to be used alongside the Hopeful Minds Overview Curriculum. We encourage you to use this program at home, in school, at church, during after-school programs, with police teaching youth programs, or anywhere where there are groups of people eager to activate hope.

No special training is required to use our Hopework book, as it was tailored for all age groups. While the book was written for anyone who can read English, parents, caregivers, or teachers may need to assist young children who are still learning to read.

Our workbook can be used with any population. We believe hope is a skill anyone and everyone should develop, as research has found hope to be impactful in many areas of life. We ALL need to know how to proactively manage hopelessness and have skills to activate hope.

The Overview is an introduction into the 'what, why, and how' of hope. We encourage you to use our Hopeful Minds Deep Dive upon completion of the Hopework book, and check out our other resources available including a Parent's Guide.

While you work through the materials, we ask that you share the images from the workbook on social media, to help us learn and inspire others on the 'how' to hope.
Tag @ifredorg @theshinehopecompany and use hashtags #HopefulMinds #Hope #ShineHope #FiveKeysToShineHope #GrowHope as you post. For our younger users, make sure to get parent permission prior to posting anything on social media. Thank you for choosing hope not only for yourself, but for those who share and teach along the way. Together, we can improve our collective future hope is key to creating all we want.

HOPE SCALES

What you cannot measure, you cannot improve. It is therefore important to measure your hope levels to monitor your progress and check in on yourself. While there are many scales for hope, we use the Children and Adult Snyder Hope Scales to measure hope, as they have been used in many studies on hope. By taking the Snyder Hope Scale regularly, you can begin to see the link between hope and outcomes in every area of your life.

Hope is a journey; as you move forward, your hope levels will rise and fall. That is okay. If you practice your hope skills regularly, no matter how hopeless life seems in the low moments, you will always have a way back to hope.

We ask that you measure your hope, and encourage all those in your community to measure hope, so we can start tracking hopefulness in individuals around the world. As you work through the Hopeful Minds curriculum, consider administering the hope scale multiple times so the students can keep track of their hope level changes.

Use the link provided to take the Snyder Hope Scale Assessment or scan the QR code below. *(with permission of legal guardian)*:

www.theshinehopecompany.com/measure-your-hope/

Children's Hope Scale

Adult Hope Scale

My current Snyder Hope Scale Score:

How do you feel about your score?

_____

_____

How hopeful have you been in your life?

_____

_____

How has your hope impacted your ability to achieve goals?

_____

_____

In what areas of your life do you feel like you could be more hopeful?

_____

_____

This course teaches you the hope skills you can use to create, maintain, and grow hope. There will be times throughout your life when you or someone you love experiences hopelessness. It is at these times, when your hope score is at its lowest, that it is most important to practice skills to activate hope.

The goal of this course is to learn the "how-to" of hope so that you can both create a model for your own life and share the power of hope with others.

Who in your life could benefit from higher hope?

_____

_____

What organizations or businesses in your community could benefit from learning about hope?

_____

_____

STRENGTHS FINDER

Understanding your strengths is another important tool for creating and maintaining hope. Focusing on your strengths can help you manage your stress response, cultivate positive thoughts, and focus on the future. Additionally, understanding strengths allows one to capitalize on their strengths while moving toward inspired actions, a necessary element in hope. Use this tool with yourself, and others. We want to focus on the children's strengths as opposed to what they are doing wrong because recognizing strengths in children can help them build confidence and support their life-long pursuit of hope. As you continue through this workbook, you will repeatedly be asked to reflect on your strengths. It is a positive way to create a more hopeful future.

You can check out your strengths here
(with permission of legal guardian):

www.hopefulmindsets.pro.viasurvey.org

Write down the top five strengths from your results:

1. _____
2. _____
3. _____
4. _____
5. _____

Which of these strengths do you think is most tied to your ability to grow and maintain hope?

_____
_____

Are you activating your strengths regularly? How so?

_____
_____

How can you better utilize your strengths at home? At work?

_____
_____

LESSON 1 WORKSHEETS

THE WHAT AND WHY OF HOPE

Please tag us on social media @ifredorg @theshinehopecompany to share your completed work and use the hashtags: #HopefulMinds #Hope #ShineHope #FiveKeysToShineHope #GrowHope #WhatAndWhyOfHope

THE HOPE MATRIX

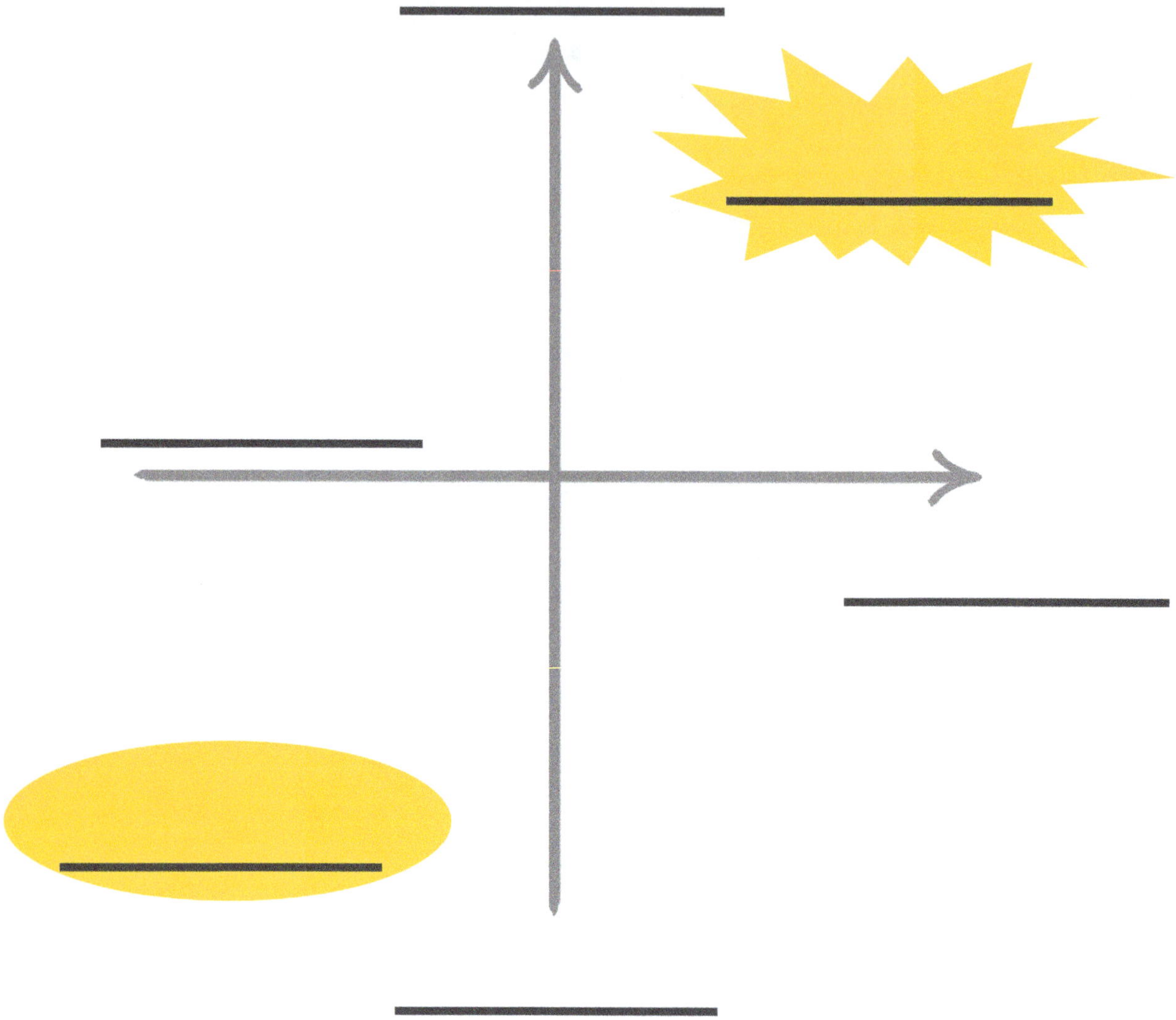

Directions: Fill in the blanks above with the following words: Hope, Hopelessness, Despair, Helplessness, Positive Feelings, Inspired Actions.

Five Keys to Shine Hope

Directions: Write the Five Keys to Shine Hope below and color the letters.

#HopefulMinds #Hope #ShineEHope #FiveKeysToShineHope #GrowHope #ShineHope

STOP. *BREATHE.* RELAX.

Directions: Circle your top four favorite stress skills from the list below. If there are additional stress skills you use that are not on the list, use the space below the add them.

Stress Skills

- 90 Second Pause
- Deep Belly Breathing
- Napping
- Calming Music
- Reaffirming beliefs
- Visualization
- Sensory Engagement
- Punching a Pillow
- Crying
- Prayer

- Walk in Nature
- Meditation
- Yoga
- Decluttering
- Focus on Strengths
- Journaling
- Exercise
- Gardening
- Time Near Water and Nature

MY FAVORITE STRESS SKILLS

-
-
-
-
-
-

-
-
-
-
-
-

HAPPINESS HABITS

Directions: Circle your top four favorite happiness habits from the list below. If there are additional happiness habits you use that are not on the list, use the space below the add them.

- Utilizing strengths
- Pursuing passion
- Activating purpose
- Smiling
- Exercising
- Playing or Listening to Music
- Spending time in Nature
- Showing Gratitude and Kindness
- Playing Games
- Volunteering
- Time with Family and Friends
- Experiencing Wonder & Awe
- Practicing Faith
- Sleeping
- Nutrition
- Dancing and Singing
- Donating
- Giving a hug
- Setting Goals
- Practicing Affirmations

My favorite happiness habits:

-
-
-
-
-
-
-

#HopefulMinds #Hope #ShineHope #FiveKeysToShineHope #GrowHope #HappinessHabits

MY HOPE SUNFLOWER

Directions: Start by filling in the sunflower's center with your definition of hope. Then, fill in the top part of the sunflower with three happiness habits that will help you remain in the upstairs brain. Finally, fill in the bottom part of the sunflower with three stress skills you can use to help when you find yourself in the downstairs brain.

Keep your face to the sunshine and you cannot see the shadow. It's what sunflowers do." -Helen Keller

LESSON 2 WORKSHEETS

EMOTIONS AND SMART ACTIONS

Please tag us on social media @ifredorg @theshinehopecompany to share your completed work and use the hashtags: #HopefulMinds #Hope #ShineHope #FiveKeysToShineHope #GrowHope #WhatAndWhyOfHope

Feelings Chart

FEELINGS WORKSHEET

Directions: Fill in each column based on the emotions on the left.

I. IDENTIFYING FEELINGS

Emotion	What does it look like?	Where do I feel it?	Where is it my brain? (circle one)
HAPPY	◯		▲ UPSTAIRS ▼ DOWNSTAIRS
ANGRY	◯		▲ UPSTAIRS ▼ DOWNSTAIRS
SAD	◯		▲ UPSTAIRS ▼ DOWNSTAIRS
SCARED	◯		▲ UPSTAIRS ▼ DOWNSTAIRS

II. MY HOPE EMOTICON

Directions: Using the space at the side, draw an emoticon for hope.

MY BRAIN

I. Directions: Fill in the blanks with the emotions of the emoticon facial expressions that match using *fear, anger, sadness, relaxed, happy,* and *excited*.

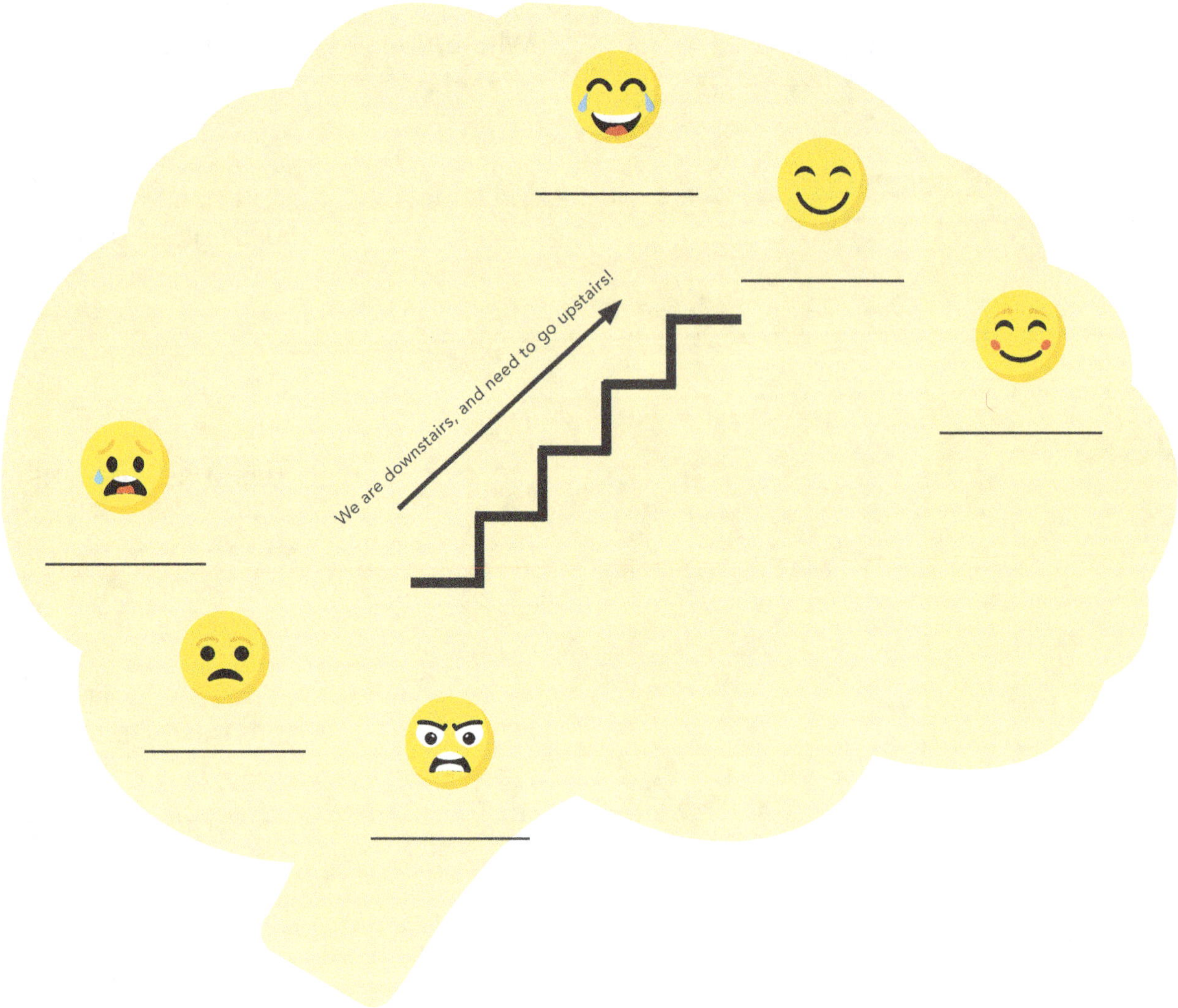

II. Directions: Draw how your body feels when you are in your upstairs and downstairs brain.

UPSTAIRS   DOWNSTAIRS

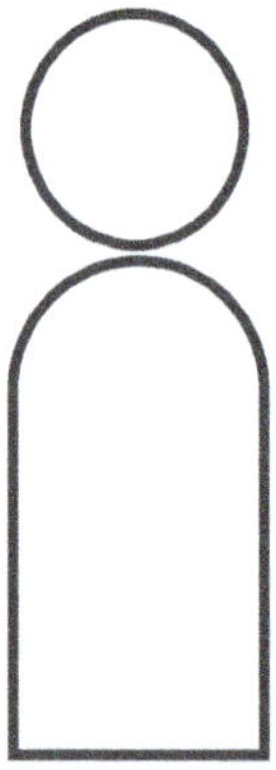

S.M.A.R.T. GOALS

Specific
Be specific about your goal. Think about these questions when creating your goal: What needs to be accomplished? Who is responsible for it? What steps will you take to achieve it?

Measurable
Can you measure your progress? If this goal will take a long time to achieve, set shorter term goals to reach along the way.

Achievable
Are you inspired and motivated to reach your goal? Do you have the tools or skills you need? If not, do you know how you can get them?

Relevant
Does your goal make sense? Does it go along with what you are trying to achieve in the bigger picture?

Time-bound
Is your timing realistic? Can you achieve your goal in the time period set? Think about what you may want to achieve at the halfway point.

INSPIRED ACTIONS

Directions: Write or draw answers to each of the prompts below.

My classroom goal this week is:

I will help myself reach my goal by:

Things that could keep me from reaching my goal:

Ways I will overcome those obstacles:

LESSON 3 WORKSHEETS

CHALLENGES TO HOPE

Please tag us on social media @ifredorg @theshinehopecompany to share your completed work and use the hashtags: #HopefulMinds #Hope #ShineHope #FiveKeysToShineHope #GrowHope #WhatAndWhyOfHope

NOURISHING NETWORK

Directions: Write or draw answers to each of the prompts below.

Friends and family I can count on and confide in:

People I turn to for Stress Skills:

People I practice Happiness Habits with:

Things I can connect to:
ex. Spiritual Advisor, Peer Support, Animals, Nature, etc.

Teachers, doctors, and experts I go to for support:

Community Resources I can utilize:

Where can I go to in times of crisis? *ex. If you can't list anyone, you can check out our list of resources for how to get connected. Visit https://hopefulcities.org/get-support/*

One person I can always count on even if we aren't close:

HOPE SUPERVILLAINS

Directions: Draw the supervillains and monsters listed in the boxes below. Write answers to the orange prompts.

Draw your HOPE Superhero

OUR HOPE HERO DEFEATS OUR HOPE VILLAINS!

I Worry About: _____

My Worry Monster:

I Ruminate On: _____

My Rumination Monster:

I Failed At: _____

My Failure Monster:

I Feel Hopelessness Because: _____

My Hopelessness Monster:

#HopefulMinds #Hope ##ShineHope #FiveKeysToShineHope #GrowHope #HopeSupervillains

CONTROL THE CONTROLLABLES

Directions: List or draw the things you CAN control in the space inside the sunflower. List or draw the things you CAN'T control in the space around the sunflower.

HOPE WORKSHEET

Directions: Fill in each box with a drawing or 1-3 sentences of writing.

Draw something you are hopeful for:

Write about what you are hopeful for:

Hope is important because:

#HopefulMinds #Hope #ShineHope #FiveKeysToShineHope #GrowHope #ImHopefulFor

MY HOPE HERO

HOW HOPEFUL ARE YOU?
Did you measure your hope? The lower your score, the more you want to practice these skills! Remember, hope is a muscle we need to build it (add it).

Check out here to get your hope score.

To write your hope hero journey, spend 20% of your time writing about their challenge, and 80% of the time sharing strategies for how they overcame it so others can learn from it. Here's how:

 1. Write your hope hero's name in the yellow line next to the box (feel free to use a nickname or anything else).

 2. Put your favorite photo of them on the yellow box, or an image of something that represents your hope hero.

 3. Write an introduction explaining the challenge they faced. Explain the two ingredients of hopelessness: despair (feelings) and helplessness (inability to act) they experienced.

 4. Share sadness, anger, fear, or other feelings, and choose 3 **Stress Skills** they used to navigate them (from the Shine infographic, or choose your own!).

 5. Share 3 **Happiness Habits** they used to get back to upstairs brain.

 6. Talk about 3 **Inspired Actions** they took, or share how your hope hero chunked down goals, the types of goals they've set, or if they had to regoal.

 7. Share who was in their **Nourishing Network**, and how it helped them navigate the challenge.

 8. Pick 3 challenges from the **'Eliminating Challenges'** on the infographic, and share how your hope hero eliminated them.

 9. Write the conclusion. What do you want the world to know? What do you wish someone had told you? What is the moral of the story?

If you're inspired, share this hope hero story so we can help activate these skills globally!

#Hope #ShineHope #MyHopeHero

> We all experience moments of hopelessness (emotional despair and motivational helplessness). The key is to use the Shine Hope skills to navigate your way from despair to positive feelings, and helplessness to inspired actions. Use the Shine Hope framework to build your muscle.

© 2024 The Shine Hope Company LLC.

MY HOPE HERO

☀ **Kathryn Goetzke**

When Kathryn was 18 years old, a freshman at the University of Iowa, her dad died by suicide. It really changed her life. When she was in her early 20's, she then tried to take her own life, yet didn't tell another soul for 10 years. She knows a lot about hopelessness.

 To work on her recovery, she used a lot of Stress Skills. She talks about crying, going to therapy, learning to meditate, deep breathing, and listening to music. She traveled a lot, and took up hiking and exercise. She also took up boxing and spent a lot of time in nature.

 Kathryn was diligent about her Happiness Habits. She listened to her favorite band the Killers, went to concerts, focused on her nutrition and sleep, and started exercising. She pursued her passions, started a nonprofit iFred, and did a lot of volunteer work. She got serious about her purpose.

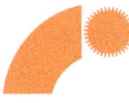 Kathryn also took a lot of Inspired Actions towards her goals. She chunked them down, got a degree and then an MBA. She couldn't talk to her dad anymore, so she found business mentors. Her brothers were always there to support her, and her mom was a source of strength and inspiration.

 Kathryn spent a lot of time with her Nourishing Networks. She spent time with people that were kind, compassionate, fun, and helped her heal. She had a therapist and got close to God. She had animals and spent a lot of time with wild horses in Nevada.

 She worked to Eliminate Challenges like her rumination and worry. She learned about sensory engagement, and even started a company to teach others. She worked to forgive herself and others. She focused on what she could control, which was her present and future, and did her best to let go of the rest. She put all her failures into teaching others.

Her use of the Shine Hope framework led her on a much healthier path. She has been sober almost 20 years, and had her nonprofit that same amount of time. She is a representative at the United Nations for the World Federation for Mental Health, and has shared her story around the world at places like the World Bank, Harvard, the United Nations, and more. She has created programming to teach hope to kids, published papers, and is now doing workplace programming, has a college, course, and is activating cities. She is on a mission to ensure all know how to hope, one person at a time. She is an inspiration, and someone that truly lives by example practicing all she teaches.

#Hope #ShineHope #MyHopeHero

MY HOPE HERO

To add image in this area, edit the PDF via Adobe Acrobat or any PDF app editor.

#Hope #ShineHope #MyHopeStory

# MY SHINE HOPE STORY™

HOW HOPEFUL ARE YOU?
Did you measure your hope? The lower your score, the more you want to practice these skills! Remember, hope is a muscle we need to build it (add it).

Check out here to get your hope score.

To write your own shine hope story, spend 20% of your time writing about your challenge, and 80% of the time sharing strategies for how you overcame it so others can learn from you. Here's how:

1. Write your name in the yellow line next to the box (feel free to use a nickname or anything else).

2. Put your favorite photo on the yellow box, or an image of something that represents you.

3. Write an introduction to your story explaining the challenge you faced. Explain the two ingredients of hopelessness: despair (feelings) and helplessness (inability to act) you experienced.

4. Share sadness, anger, fear, or other feelings, and choose **3 Stress Skills** you used to naviate them (from the Shine infographic, or choose your own!).

5. Share **3 Happiness Habits** you used to get back to your upstairs brain.

6. Talk about **3 Inspired Actions** you took, or share how you chunked down goals, the types of goals you set, or if you had to regoal.

7. Share who was in your **Nourishing Network**, and how they helped you navigate the challenge.

8. Pick 3 challenges from the **'Eliminating Challenges'** on the infographic, and share how you eliminated them.

9. Write your conclusion. What do you want the world to know? What do you wish someone had told you? What is the moral of the story?

If you're inspired, share your story so we can help activate these skills globally.

#Hope #ShineHope #MyShineHopeStory

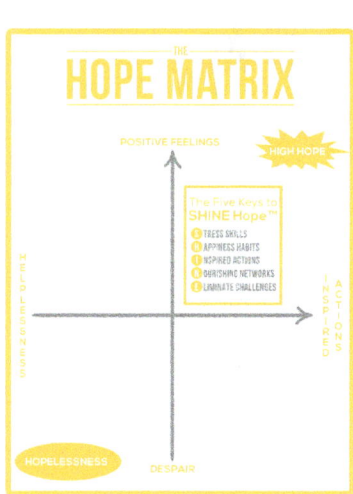

We all experience moments of hopelessness (emotional despair and motivational helplessness). The key is to use the Shine Hope skills to navigate your way from despair to positive feelings, and helplessness to inspired actions. Use the Shine Hope framework to build your muscle.

© 2024 The Shine Hope Company LLC.

MY SHINE HOPE STORY™

☀ Kathryn Goetzke

When I was 18 years old, a freshman at the University of Iowa, I called home and heard an unfamiliar, deep voice on the other line. It wasn't anyone I recognized, and he asked for my mom. My mom got on the phone to tell me my dad had taken his life. In that instance, my whole world crumbled. I felt a sadness so deep I thought I would never survive, and a helplessness so profound as I could not bring him back.

As hard as it was, I had to move forward. I started using Stress Skills to manage my pain. I cried when I was sad, started boxing to manage my anger, and learned how to start belly breathing to manage my fear. I listened to a lot of calming music when things got hard, and I started hiking all over the world. I also learned how to use sensory engagement to bring myself to the present moment.

Happiness Habits were critical. Sleep became an important part of my routine, and I started eating healthier foods. I cut alcohol out of my life. I replaced smoking with running, and made comedy clubs and laughter a part of my life. I listened to music, turned my sensory engagement passion into a purpose and started a company, and made volunteering a regular part of my life. I used dancing and live concerts (like my fave The Killers) as a form of release.

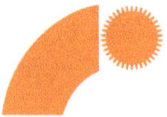

I also was very intentional about Inspired Actions. I had to chunk down my goals, leaving school and taking only one year at a time until I graduated. I had to regoal from having experiences with my dad to finding father-like figures to be in my life. I got closer to my brothers, their kids, and found mentors like Paul Carter and Dr. Belfer to guide me on my journey. My mom is my rock, my greatest source of strength and inspiration, keeping me moving forward towards my dreams.

Nourishing Networks were a constant. I stayed close to my friends and family, traveling, dancing, studying, and laughing. They were so compassionate, kind, generous, fun, and helped me heal. I forgave my dad for leaving, and forgave myself for not being there for him when he needed me. I got very close to God, understanding that I couldn't save my dad, and that in time this lesson would teach me how to help others.

It wasn't easy to Eliminate Challenges like rumination, internalizing failure, or worry. Yet I studied sensory engagement to be present when my mind started running. I deconstructed what led to my dad taking his life in a way that made it clear how to save myself and others. I knew that I couldn't control my dad, just like I can't control others. So I have focused on creating programming yet not being attached to if people want to learn it.

It's not been the easiest journey, and takes work. Yet by using the Shine Hope framework I have created a new life that is full of wonder, awe, happiness, adventure, and meaning. A different one than I expected, yet a beautiful one because I was able to dive in my pain, and learn the lessons necessary to teach others. And I use all my dad taught me in business to create a Shine Hope model for the world that ensures all know the what, why, and how of hope. And for that I know he is so very proud.

No matter what life brings, Keep Shining.

#Hope #ShineHope #MyHopeStory

© 2024 The Shine Hope Company LLC.

MY SHINE HOPE STORY™

#Hope #ShineHope #MyHopeStory
© 2024 The Shine Hope Company LLC.

WHAT FUELS MY HOPE?

Hopeful Minds

Spread Hope. Tag us on social media @ifredorg @theshinehopecompany and use hashtags #HopefulMinds #Hope #ShineHope #FiveKeysToShineHope #GrowHope #Hopefuel

WHAT AM I HOPEFUL FOR?

Hopeful Minds

Spread Hope. Tag us on social media @ifredorg @theshinehopecompany and use hashtags #HopefulMinds #Hope #ShineHope #FiveKeysToShineHope #GrowHope #ImHopefulFor

MY HOPE JOURNAL

1. How are you using your hope tools to succeed? Think about the SHINE acronym and how you've used it.

2. How has hope helped you overcome obstacles?

3. What SMART goals do you have for the future?

4. What can you control about the school year? What can't you control? How can you make the most of what they can control? How can you release emotions from what they can't control? How can you be creative about their experience this semester or year?

5. How do you define a hero? What do you think are some of the qualities in a hero? How does this person use hope tools in their life?

Please tag us on social media @ifredorg @theshinehopecompany to share your completed work and use the hashtags: #HopefulMinds #Hope #ShineHope #FiveKeysToShineHope #GrowHope #WhatAndWhyOfHope

MY HOPE JOURNAL

MY HOPE JOURNAL

MY HOPE JOURNAL

www.ingramcontent.com/pod-product-compliance
Lightning Source LLC
Chambersburg PA
CBHW081511080526
44589CB00017B/2725